Riding for
the ECK Brand

Also by Harold Klemp

This book has been authored by and published under the supervision of the Mahanta, the Living ECK Master, Sri Harold Klemp. It is the Word of ECK.

MAHANTA

Riding for the ECK Brand

The Living ECK Master Speaks to the High Initiates

Harold Klemp

ᘓK

ECKANKAR
Minneapolis
www.Eckankar.org

Riding for the ECK Brand

Printed in USA
Library of Congress Control Number: 91-76119
ISBN: 978-1-57043-023-7
Third printing—2008

Compiled from the talks of Sri Harold Klemp
by Mary Carroll Moore
Edited by Joan Klemp and Anthony Moore
Cover Illustration by Roy Kerswill
Illustrations by Kevin McMahon
Text photo (page viii) by Robert Huntley
Back cover photo by Robert Huntley

∞ This paper meets the requirements of ANSI/NISO Z39.48-1992 (Permanence of Paper).

Contents

Sri Harold Klemp, the Mahanta, the Living ECK Master brings you a greater understanding of your role within the spiritual hierarchy.

Introduction

The Brothers of the Leaf means all for one and one for all. And the only way this can happen is when the walls of fear, illusion, and materialism are pushed back. The only way ECK can come into this world is through Its channels, and this means through you.

We say ECK sustains all life, and It does. But when It's working for the upliftment of Soul, It works through the spiritual hierarchy. The ECK comes through you as Its channel, and just by being around you, others wonder why you are different.

When the love of the SUGMAD begins to come through the Brothers of the Leaf in a greater way, you will see changes. We'll begin acting with more common sense, with a greater bond of unity. We'll be doing things that work. It's because of the love of the SUGMAD that the Brothers of the Leaf are going to grow and build.

Don't be halfhearted. If you're not carrying your own weight, someone else is going to have to carry it for you.

1

Riding for the Brand—
The Community of Brothers

The concept of riding for the brand was big in the American West. It was the idea of one for all and all for one.

This meant that when a cowboy signed up to work for a ranch, he fully supported that ranch. He was totally loyal to the brand in every way. If he couldn't agree with the ranch policies, the cowboy would give notice, pack his things, and leave. There were no hard feelings: It was just how it was.

Your Wholehearted Support

Being a Brother of the Leaf is very much like being a cowboy of the old West who rode for a certain brand. If you're for it, by all means ride for the brand. But don't be halfhearted. If you're not carrying your own weight, someone else is going to have to carry it for you. That wasn't appreciated in the old West and it's not appreciated now.

If you're going to be in ECK, if you're going to be part of the Brothers of the Leaf, support it wholeheartedly. If you would do something for the Mahanta, do as much for each other. This will make the love bond stronger. It will also take care of many of the petty jealousies that can arise.

People who don't carry their weight in ECK find themselves gradually backing away from the heart center. They lose touch with the Ocean of Love and Mercy. They begin to find all kinds of compelling reasons why they're being driven away—psychic attacks and such things. But the fact is they're allowing it to happen themselves.

Tearing Down Inner Walls

When the Iron Curtain came down, we had to look at what it meant within ECKANKAR. It meant that we had to begin to bring down the walls between us, walls that could have been put up by initiates of the highest levels. In order to carry the message of ECK to the world, we're going to have to tear down these walls that stand between us as initiates.

It's one of those painful subjects we'd rather not talk about. We think, If there are walls, they are put up by other people. Or, If I have a wall, there's a good reason for it. We can look down our noses at someone else, but it's always good to look at ourselves first.

Cultivate Humility

Sometimes we don't understand why another person is so bent over from carrying a load. It seems to us that he is carrying an ordinary bag of groceries. But at times each of us carries spiritual loads many times heavier than any other human being can know.

A person can feel like a total failure under such a

load. He may say, "I am struggling so; I must not be fit for the position the Mahanta has given me." This isn't true at all. If you can just hold on a little longer—sometimes for even twenty minutes or an hour more—help will come. Help always comes, no matter how badly you think you're doing.

Sometimes you are thrown into situations where your personal training, abilities, or strength is totally inadequate. If you rely on only your own powers, you are going to fail. It's a lesson in humility. If it were not for the presence of the Inner Master, you would be powerless to bring any kind of benefit to the person with a problem, yourself or anyone else.

Unless you are humble before God, the SUGMAD, humble before the ECK and the Mahanta, you will find it impossible to be a clear channel for the divine power. But if you are open, you will find that you have all of the protection and love which is needed for whatever you are facing at that moment.

Dealing with Clay Feet

I look back to the early days of ECKANKAR, and I see how difficult it was for Paul Twitchell. But I also see how he had certain advantages. For one thing, he could talk about the high state of the Mahdis. Since there were so few Mahdis scattered all over the globe, it was unlikely that anyone ever saw one, and more importantly never saw their clay feet.

When you hit a low, when you are reminded of your clay feet, this is a good time to have another Brother of the Leaf around. A person at the bottom doesn't need someone reading the riot act to him: "You know why this happened to you; you got exactly what was coming." It's important to use tact and love and diplomacy with your fellow Brothers.

Spend time with other Higher Initiates. It's wonderful to share something in a spiritual way with other Brothers of the Leaf. This strengthens the love bond within the community of Brothers. We can get to know each other as people, yet work within the spiritual worlds.

Often I meet people when I'm out shopping or at the library. Looking at them, I ask myself, Are these the kind of people I would like in ECK? Usually I say, Yes, these are good people. I would hope that an ECKist who gets the Fifth Initiation would be at least as good a person.

2

Becoming a Higher Initiate

Often I meet people when I'm out shopping or at the library. Looking at them, I ask myself, Are these the kind of people I would like in ECK? Usually I say, Yes, these are good people. I would hope an ECKist who gets the Fifth Initiation would be at least as good a person.

Generally I will give the Fifth to an individual when he has shown enough spiritual initiative to be willing to accept more of the responsibility for his spiritual life.

What It Means to Be a Higher Initiate

The higher we go, the more stable we become spiritually. We also become more open and flexible. When something comes up and doesn't work out the way we want it to, we're more willing to look for alternative plans.

Spiritually, the purpose of the lower worlds is for us to learn to work together and become Co-workers with God. Unless we learn how to work together, we cannot become Co-workers with God.

Sometimes a person thinks he is so right about something and everyone else is so wrong. He is really saying, As Soul, I am greater than these people. Spiritually, I am greater than these other Souls.

If we have any understanding at all about spiritual matters, we realize that Soul is Soul. In the Ocean of Love and Mercy, Soul equals Soul.

Balance and the Higher Initiations

I want to make sure that the people who become Higher Initiates are worthy of it. I want to be sure they have a chance of continuing to be Higher Initiates. But it's always a bit of a gamble.

Being imbalanced is one of the most serious reasons why a person doesn't get the Fifth Initiation right away. Someone who has problems with drugs or gets out of balance in any number of different ways can cause problems for other chelas. When a person shows an imbalance, I like to proceed very slowly.

A Fourth Initiate waits six years to come into the Fifth Circle. If he's ready, he's given the initiation; if not, he waits at least another year or two.

Once a person gets the Fifth Initiation, I generally let at least two years pass before I may ask him to serve as clergy. He needs time to become used to the Fifth Circle. After a few more years, I may invite him to serve as an Initiator, then later maybe an ECK Spiritual Aide.

Being a Co-worker

There's a distinction between being a Co-worker with the Mahanta and being a Co-worker with God. Being a

Co-worker with the Mahanta is the practice that you do for one day becoming a Co-worker with God.

A Co-worker with God is an ECK Master who knows what needs to be done and how to work in harmony with all beings in the hierarchy of the Vairagi Masters—just by being in contact with the SUGMAD Realization. Co-workers with the Mahanta are learning how to do that.

Allowing Others Freedom

An executive dean of a Texas college was flying to another city for training. On the plane she met a young engineer. He was project director for a large engineering company. He admitted to her that his training in engineering had not prepared him for administrative duties. Since she had been in management for many years and knew how to run an organization, they talked quite a bit.

As they discussed their jobs, the ECKist had the feeling that the engineer was really asking for some kind of spiritual help. She knew this even though his questions were about management techniques. So she changed the subject and began telling him little stories about her children.

The conversation moved to how one of her children had been out of the body at some point. Suddenly the young engineer said, "I just remembered. I was out of the body when I was a child." She said, "You were?" He said, "Yes, but I've never felt comfortable talking about it." The woman replied, "I understand completely. It's very important to be considerate of other people's comfort zones."

As they parted at the airport, the engineer had a big smile on his face. Talking with this woman had given him the understanding that there were other people in very prestigious positions who recognized and understood such things as being out of the body.

Right Arm of the Mahanta

As a Higher Initiate you are on the front line of the spiritual wave. How can you be a right arm of the Mahanta? Sometimes the best way to be a right arm of the Mahanta is to allow people to have their space, such as this woman did with the engineer.

The engineer knew he had been out of the body. Up until then he had always thought the body was himself. But if he wasn't the body, who was he? Being out of the body presupposes that Soul is the mover. There was a spiritual question here that the engineer hadn't quite the awareness to define at this point. The H.I. had sparked it within him. The understanding will come to him in time.

As the right arm of the Mahanta, you are often put into positions where you can't always talk about ECK. So you just listen to what people are saying. This is one of the ways you can serve.

Karmic Spin-off

At an ECK seminar, I asked a friend how he had slept the night before. He said it had been kind of rough. He had woken up with a fever blister. I said, "That's odd. I woke up with a fever blister too."

He told me he usually got them when a lot of things were going on on the inner planes. At seminar time, karma is speeded up for some people, and it spins off. Higher Initiates help take care of some of this spin-off.

Active Vehicles

Many people feel that the closer you get to God-Realization, the more you sit on your duff. You sit back, you talk big, and you have profound thoughts. But actually the higher you go, the harder you work.

Some people say they have had a high spiritual experience. They go to the top of the mountain, but then they retreat to an ashram. What good is their experience then? It's like putting a space capsule full of people in outer space. If it never comes back to earth, some very precious cargo is lost. A cycle isn't completed.

Creating Your Own Worlds

Life continues to be very interesting after the Fifth Initiation, as you continue to unfold further in the Light and Sound.

In the worlds of the Fifth Plane and above, you learn to create your own worlds. You don't always have someone looking over your shoulder, giving you directions. You won't gain your own Mastership if someone else is always pulling the strings.

You have to find out how the ECK works with you in the higher worlds. Does It give you gentle nudges, or do you get a sense of knowing? Or does someone come along and give you an idea just at the right moment?

Remember that we have the element of free will in ECK. Even though the Master may see your potential, even though he gives you the opportunity to exercise that potential and become a greater spiritual being, it still depends upon you.

There is such a mystique around different elements in the ECKANKAR organization, especially the higher initiations. Some people even believe that Higher Initiates can walk on water. When Fourth Initiates become new Fifths, I hope they don't try it and end up at the bottom of the lake.

As a person learns how to work within a group, he silently carries a different vibration of Light and Sound. Other people can feel this. They respond to it more than any actions that individual might carry out.

3
Working Together

The countries of Europe have been at each other's throats for many centuries. This is not a problem with Europe per se; it's a problem of the human consciousness. Human beings have been fighting wars against each other for a long time.

If cooperation can develop between the separate units of Europe, there may not have to be another major war among the people in that area of the world.

We know this is a warring universe. But as mankind unfolds spiritually, people are going to have to learn to work with their neighbors again. We're not looking for peace in a warring universe; we are learning how to work together. Unless we do, we cannot become Co-workers with God.

How to Work in Harmony with Others

Sometimes I've found I learn more doing something the way someone else has suggested. When people tell me, "We respect your opinion, but we strongly recommend something else," then I have to consider their comments. I think the wisest person is the one who listens to the good judgments of others. A successful leader isn't someone who knows everything, but he does have the wisdom to know who has the right answers.

As a person learns how to work within a group, he silently carries a different vibration of Light and Sound. Other people can feel this. They respond to it more than any actions that individual might carry out.

Having the Light and Sound in your life means you'll be working more cooperatively with other people in ECKANKAR. This doesn't mean there isn't room for dissent; there are forums in ECK for dissent. At meetings, everyone has a say in the matter, but then a decision is made. If you win, great. If you lose, you make a better argument next time. That's how it works.

Until you are balanced within the group, you usually find your actions are counterproductive.

Avoiding Power Trips

We are looking to spread the message of ECK. The only people who can do this well are those who are clear channels for the ECK. And we can't be clear channels when we're on a power trip. It's just impossible.

Sometimes we're more in tune with ECK than at other times. When we're out of tune, we can do a lot of damage to people who are sensitive in their spiritual unfoldment.

Sometimes a person making psychic attacks on others is unconscious of it. The easiest thing to do when you see this is to go running to the ECKANKAR Spiritual Center. But if we can start by talking to each other and trying to work it out, we'll be a lot happier. Then the ECKANKAR Spiritual Center won't start controlling more than necessary.

Some people don't really understand there is a greater mission than power politics. When I work with people, they give me their opinion or ideas on a plan. Then once we have agreed on something, everybody supports it, whether it was his idea or not. We work within a hierarchy. The final decision has to be in the hands of one person.

Sometimes you may agree with the RESA, and other times you may not. If you cannot agree at all, it's best to just let the situation be and step back. The RESA is not more or less sanctified, pure, or holy than anyone else. The RESA just makes sure that whatever plan the group sets out to do is in keeping with the spiritual principles of ECK.

We have something much more important to accomplish than building our own little castles. There are a lot of people waiting for the message of ECK, waiting for the Light and Sound of God.

Unfoldment

Unfoldment cannot take place in a vacuum. We have to be with people. And if we're going to be with people who have karmic problems the way we do, there will be sparks. So we have to learn how to work together.

Maybe a person is on a council, and the members are having a difficult time getting along. Karma is worked off in this process, not just by the outer interaction, but by the mere fact that they are on a council together. A council has its own vibration. The dregs of the past come to the surface to be resolved.

Sometimes I think the real purpose of it all is for people to come into balance with each other. After they do that, they may get some work done.

Choosing a Larger Consciousness

Often the ECK arranges it so the very answers we need come from people we can't stand. This is what makes being a leader so hard. So few people have enough wisdom to put aside their judgments of personality and look to the substance of an issue. Very few can overlook personal conflicts and accept an idea on its own merit.

If you have the spiritual awareness to have good people around you—those who love ECK, even if they don't agree with you—you will get all the help you need to make the very best decisions. But if you select only the people whose opinions you like, you probably have chosen a very small consciousness of life because it's no larger than your own.

Consciousness extends to the very extremes of life. The SUGMAD has created all life and loves all life, from one end of the scale to the other. Within that all-encompassing range are all states of consciousness.

Process versus Product

ECKists have something in them that makes them want to excel in whatever they do. But many ECKists need to learn that the product isn't as important as the process of achieving harmony.

As soon as you have harmony within a group, you have concentrated effort. Then you'll find that any project gets carried out very quickly and smoothly. You'll also find that when people in a group work out their differences, some will naturally move into other positions.

This is how the ECK works. There isn't an end goal, except the process of reaching a goal. Life is important, not the fact that you've lived it.

Inner or Outer Guidance?

People sometimes say to me: "I'm an ECKist, and I have inner guidance. My inner guidance tells me to do something the RESA has told me not to do."

We have to understand something about this: On earth, neither the chela nor the RESA is absolutely correct. But within the spiritual administration the RESA is my representative in an area. The RESAs make the best decisions they can.

As leaders in ECK, it isn't effective to come on as the authority, saying, "Do it this way because I told you to." It isn't effective in ECKANKAR because we work with individuals as Soul. Many of them are going to earn their way into the higher initiations. They're nobody's fool; neither were we.

Part of the secret to working together is listening. If someone comes up to you, listen to his ideas. Listen without forming any judgments. Then if you need clarification, ask questions. Spiritual discipline is learning to work with those we find it hardest to work with.

We're to the stage where we can accept each other in the spirit of love as Brothers of the Leaf. If good ideas come up, we can work with each other and help each other. We look, we learn, we ask for information. We're not too proud to ask or admit that somebody else may have the answer.

Reaching Our Spiritual Level

At some point we reach our spiritual level. Then some feel that ECKANKAR has no more to offer them. To be honest, I'd say it's generally because of pride.

I expect a fallout of Higher Initiates as we move along. New initiates believe that Higher Initiates walk on water. They don't walk on water, and some of them fall into the depths. If there are problems with the outer organization, they suddenly say, "I'm going to become inner-directed. I'm only going to listen to what my heart says." They assume that what they hear from the inner channels needs no outer direction or correction.

Historically the ECK teachings are built upon an Inner and Outer Master, inner and outer teachings. People who have just an inner teaching often don't realize they need something on the outside as a measure or standard to tell them where they are.

When people say they're going to just follow their hearts and forget about the organization, they've chosen an unbalanced path. The path of ECK is balanced because it has the outer and the inner teachings. These people are not competent enough to go only on the inner teachings and make the most direct progress back to the high worlds of the SUGMAD. But they don't know it, do they?

Balanced Self-Sufficiency

When I first worked in a printing department I thought I had to be self-sufficient. And being self-sufficient, I had to know all the answers. A lot of times, I went way out in left field by myself. Then management would come along and say, "Cool it," and I'd have to get smart real quick.

All the answers are not accessible to us at all times because of the worries of the day. We may not always be able to go to the Inner Master and say, "What do I do in this situation?" Sometimes the pressures of the day close out this avenue. When this happens, we can remember to talk to another Higher Initiate who may be more open.

There were times when some of us were the only Higher Initiates in an area. Other ECKists flocked to us. We became the authority. When more Higher Initiates finally came into the area, we hadn't yet developed the practice of asking others for help. A question would come along, and we'd figure the answer must be within ourselves. So we did the best we could. Sometimes in a very specific area, such as public relations, we didn't have the knowledge to approach a radio or television station. But maybe one of the other initiates did.

If we get into the habit of practicing coworkership, we recognize we don't know all things. Asking another person to help also gives him a chance to contribute and grow. It can bring new life to a Satsang, and we can learn from this person. We need the help of many other people in life, and not just those who are Higher Initiates.

No Longer an Itinerant Teaching

These are wonderful times we're seeing. The Temple of ECK is a place of permanence, as permanent as a place can be on earth. It gives us a certain amount of recognition that we need to reach people with the Light and Sound of ECK. We simply haven't had it until now.

People don't take you seriously unless you have a home. If you're a wanderer, a hobo, it's every man for himself. You ride the rails, you hit the trail, but it's just you. It's the individual aspect of the teachings. It's not the aspect of coworkership.

The group consciousness of ECK has been changing in the last few years toward coworkership. The Temple of ECK is going to bring this out even more. It's only through coworkership that ECKANKAR and the teachings of ECK can actually become important in the lives of many people. We've gotten as much mileage as we can as an itinerant teaching. Now we have to take another step.

Because people say, "Don't go so fast," I wait as long as I can before taking the next step. It's very hard to make a change. ECKists come from all cultures and countries. Trying to keep all the chelas moving forward with their vision on the SUGMAD and God Consciousness is not easy, especially when they look back and say, "I want things the way they were before."

I know what they're talking about, but let's not stop and smell the roses too long. Smell them for a little while, then move on. The heavens higher up are always prettier, more beautiful, and more enjoyable.

Spiritual Realization and God-Realization are only big principles that mean nothing to a person until he, himself, has experienced them. When he does, he suddenly knows what I'm talking about. When it comes through, a person's life is changed. All these realizations we're having about ourselves through dreams and Soul Travel should tell us more about the present, to show us who and what we are today.

People coming into ECK these days ask the Arahata,
"How can you relate the ECK teachings to my life today?"

4

Service—
Sharing ECK with Others

There is a force inside each individual that he consciously has no control over. It's the call of Soul. It is Soul hearing the Music of God. It constantly pushes him to find the answer. He knows it is not in this world.

Although Soul may be having experiences with this Music, or Voice, of God, the outer side of the individual, the human being, is often not aware of it. He may just have a feeling that there is more to life than what he has in his present religion. So he begins to search through different philosophies. He is searching for truth.

Search for Truth

An initiate was flying from the United States to Australia for an ECK seminar. He sat beside a woman who had an Australian accent. Since he was visiting Australia for the first time, he asked her about Perth, the city where the seminar would be. It turned out to be her hometown, so she talked to him for a while. At one point, she asked about the book he was reading, *Soul Travelers of the Far Country.*

He said it was written by the Living ECK Master and it was about Soul and Its journey through this world. Then he told her about HU.

The Australian woman began listing the great number of spiritual paths she had been on. She said that in every path she had looked for a certain element of truth but she couldn't find it. She told the initiate, "I've looked for truth in this life, but I haven't found it." She had quit all religions and written off this lifetime. The woman was only living out the rest of a bleak experience, until she sat next to the ECKist on the plane that day and heard about the HU.

Updated Approaches to Sharing God

People coming into ECK these days have a different perspective about life and living than in years past. They are more interested in knowing what the ECK teachings can do for them now. They ask the Arahata, "How can you relate the ECK teachings to my life today?"

This is not easy to do because the people who come to ECK classes usually bring orthodox religious thought with them. This has to be melted away very slowly. It sometimes takes years before it melts enough to where an intelligent spiritual conversation is possible.

Our method of teaching ECKANKAR is evolving. Those of you who are good teachers now find that people actually like to come to Satsang class, where it used to be such drudgery.

When I was in my first years in ECK, I taught a number of Satsang classes. Back then, I would have a person read one paragraph of the discourse, then we would discuss it. Maybe somebody said something;

maybe nobody said anything. So I'd move on to the next paragraph. When I look back at some of the things I did in my first years, I cringe.

We're trying to develop a teaching program where the ECK initiates will want to come to class and will grow spiritually from the experience. After all, why have Satsang if this doesn't happen?

I know that everybody likes philosophical discussions. They make you feel good. But I also know that teaching by stories and parables will reach people better than pure philosophy.

If you select stories carefully, the ECK principles are embodied in them. It's just Soul having the experience of life. Like eating an artichoke, life can be a frustrating experience, but you keep peeling off the outer leaves because there's going to be something worthwhile in there somewhere.

We need to be simple and up-to-date with newcomers to ECK. Conditions are changing very fast karmically. As they change, we must change with them so that we respond to the spiritual needs of people who come to ECKANKAR. Instead of having them conform to a structure that we set up in the past, we have to serve the spiritual needs of the people as they are today.

A Higher Initiate was telling me that people make up their minds faster now. They know within themselves that ECK is what they want, so they may come to only twelve weeks of a discussion class and immediately become a chela. They see they can work into God-Realization from this. Their primary interest is in going home to God.

When times get harder, people are driven back to God. It's the silver lining in the cloud during the hard times.

Using Discrimination

In their efforts to present ECK to people, initiates will be coming to you for approval of all sorts of projects and ideas. Some of them sound good. They sound exactly like what is needed to attract new people, and maybe they will.

But we don't want to reach people at all costs. We want to reach the right people. If the super-phenomenal aspects of ECKANKAR get newcomers in the door, they will want to know where all the glitter went when they find out that ECKANKAR is something different. Worse than not getting enough of the right people is getting too many of the wrong ones.

Talk with the Inner Master and with each other when an idea is proposed that sends ripples over your skin. Not the goose bumps which are usually good, but ripples that run over the skin in waves, where you just feel uncomfortable and want to talk it over with someone else.

We constantly do this at the office too. As a plan is set in motion, we have checkpoints where we can adjust it. I often ask someone to come up with a preliminary plan or idea. Then I can make suggestions.

Putting ECK into Writing

In the late sixties and early seventies, people were interested in psychic subjects. So what did Paul Twitchell do? He wrote about psychic subjects. He worked with people where they were at, and when he got their attention, he lifted them beyond the psychic worlds.

Paul had a typist who didn't particularly care about the ECK works. She just typed by the hour. He knew that his writings needed editing, but he once said that it was such a drain to get the stuff out the first time, he didn't want to see it again.

Paul never meant to make the ECK writings obscure, but he took exceedingly difficult thoughts from the ethers and brought them out here. The thoughts Paul had are still powerful, but it takes time to unravel what he was trying to say. Looking through some of his discourses, I'm often surprised that you understood them, that you're still in ECK.

Trying to update Paul's writings drives me up the wall sometimes. I joke that I've put footprints all over the ceiling and walls as I try to follow one of his thoughts. Sometimes I work for an hour or two on a single paragraph. When you're editing, you have to get inside the writer's head and go into contemplation again and again.

It's like making soap on the farm. You get yourself a big pot, you get a fire going underneath it, then you throw in lard and lye. Everything boils, and you stir it a lot. Finally you come out with good homemade soap. It's the same with editing, with life. It's got to go through the furnace. That's the only way purification occurs.

You don't get credit for making something obscure. We edited the discourses simply to open them up and make the ECK teachings simpler for others. People will come into ECK when they can understand it.

The people today are not the same kind of people that we had in 1965 or 1970. A Second Initiate today is going to be at a higher state of consciousness than a Second Initiate in 1965. The Mahanta Consciousness keeps expanding. If it holds true for the Mahanta, it also holds true for the initiates.

Keeping Up with ECK

Because people coming into ECK today have a higher state of consciousness, they're sharp. They have different questions and different needs, and you have to answer them. It's not good enough to stop growing, to rest in the consciousness of 1970. You'd be left behind.

A Second Initiate at the time of Christ was at a very different level than a Second Initiate is today. Higher Initiates who left ECK eight or ten years ago may still consider themselves ECKists. But if they wanted to become active today, they might be at the level of a Second Initiate. While they rested, there has been a general upliftment of consciousness.

Truth is always the same, but the manner in which you present it is constantly changing. Somehow you have to find ways to meet the expanding consciousness. And if you're going to keep up, you'll be expanding in consciousness too.

I like to direct people to the Inner Master. If they have trouble with that, the spiritual exercises will bridge the gap.

Working with the Living Word

Sometimes when I go to the library, it's so oppressive that I get a headache. It's somebody else's knowledge compiled in shelves and shelves of books. Even when I'm going through ECK history, it can seem so flat. How do you liven it up? How do you speak about the Living Word? You bring in more of the Light and Sound.

If you're fortunate enough to find someone who wants to know more about ECK, don't talk his ear off. To make him more comfortable, tell him that ECK is simply something to help Soul in Its journey home to God. It's this and nothing more. It works through the twin aspects of Sound and Light.

At times people are so filled with the Light and Sound of ECK and so filled with love that they want to go out and tell everyone about ECK. But sometimes telling's not as smart as listening. Just by being with people, listening to them more than telling, the ECK will help you. If there's to be a conversation, the ECK will help you know what to say.

Serving Wherever You Are

A Higher Initiate worked with the Salvation Army. It was her way of making a living, but she wondered if it was OK. How could she serve ECK in a Christian organization?

I said, "Do what you can. Teach what you can about the ECK principles, but don't offend the people by using our terms outwardly. Do what you can in your own quiet way."

That's what she's doing. Once she's served her time there, the ECK will give her another way to make a living. If the job you have now is the only way you can make a living, it's probably because the ECK wants you to do something with that group of people.

The Aspirant Program

The teachings of ECK come to uplift religions, not to destroy them. This means that as ECK initiates we sometimes serve among people who are still in other religions. Higher Initiates who go to church with their parents know that while their parents can't understand

31

ECKANKAR, they are still learning something from the example of their son or daughter who is an H.I.

The ECK teachings are also for the aspirant, a broad group which takes in many people and many different levels of commitment to ECK. It includes people who believe in ECK, who follow ECK, but who are not able to commit themselves in the way those of the inner circles can.

Celebrations of Life

When Christianity was young, it was a breath of fresh air to people who had outgrown the pagan religions. Today it's easy for us to be critical of Christianity for borrowing festivals from the pagan religions. Over the centuries, Christianity tried to hide the origin of these festivals because it did not strengthen or advance Christianity.

Christianity took the old religions and turned them upside down. As time goes on, a religion like this itself becomes like a basket turned upside down. It shuts out the light. Someone has to come along and, through the direction of the ECK, turn the basket right side up. Then the light can shine back into the activities of people and their celebrations of life.

Meeting People Halfway

A Higher Initiate from New Zealand talked with me about what people were responding to. Seekers in her immediate area weren't very interested in Soul Travel, while those farther south were. The people in her area worked in hospice programs because they wanted to help others. The people farther south liked more of the higher mental truths like spiritual unfoldment and enlightenment. Any one region might have four or five sectors where the spiritual needs are entirely different.

Do we expect someone to make a huge jump from wherever they are, or do we meet them halfway? First we find out what they're used to. You'll find that people will come to ECK when you meet their needs. But you have to find out what their needs are, and that's very hard.

A few years ago I noticed the competition for the ECK initiates' time in today's fast-paced world. I realized if I wanted to get the ECK message across, I would have to refine it greatly and condense it so they could get the essential message.

When I shortened my seminar talks, I had to regear my entire thought process, trying to make the ECK message fit in a shorter time period. Thus in my talks I now focus on a key point, using the sharpest images possible, so that the message will basically go from the heart of ECK to the heart of the chela—the most direct transfer possible.

Right now our biggest move to try and answer the spiritual needs of people worldwide is the position of RESA. The RESA is a more direct agent of the Living ECK Master than we've ever established in the past. It gives us flexibility, like having a Spiritual Services department in ninety-two countries around the globe.

Cycles of Growth and Cycles of Consolidation

We go into a growth cycle, then a consolidation cycle, then a growth cycle again. During the periods of consolidation, you may wonder why people don't want to hear more about ECK. Remember to take it step-by-step. The work you put in isn't lost; it will bear fruit in its season.

When you ask, Are we failing or something? remember you're not failing. You are just a reflection of what is happening at the very heart of ECK. During the consolidation periods people look very hard at themselves and ask if ECK is really for them. It's a kind of shakeout period.

Keep working at it. You're planting the seeds. Maybe it will be a while before you see results; maybe the next guy will get the credit. But you're putting the word out, and people are watching and studying you to see if you're honest and ethical, a good person.

Growth just takes a long time, but we've made a beginning. Some of the fruits are showing already. Through the RESAs, the ECKists have direction at home in how to present the message of ECK to people. It's like a wave that's building momentum. And as it builds, the RESAs are going to need your support.

Sometimes we hold the ECK teachings too dear to ourselves. It's very natural. We say, This is how it used to be done when Paul Twitchell did it. What we are actually saying is I've become frozen in consciousness.

The ECK is a living thing which moves forward. It's constantly expanding, but we sometimes find ourselves reluctant to expand with It. We have to draw upon new creativity within ourselves, and this involves effort. It's very hard to come up with the energy to push ourselves into new areas of unfoldment.

Spiritual Bridge-Building

Whenever a spiritual teaching comes out into the mainstream, it always builds upon what went before.

It builds on common human experience.

For example, mankind has always wondered about what goes on on the other side. Where do dreams come from? What happens to a person when the body lies down at translation? These questions have been bothering mankind from the first.

A spiritual teaching is worthless unless it relates to the people it's supposed to reach. If it's too foreign, it doesn't relate to people's needs. Then it's useless.

To make a bridge to people, we begin with dreams. Dreams and Soul Travel are generally the bridges which will take a person from the lower to the higher worlds.

To answer their questions, we've created little cells of ECK energy. One is the HU Chant; another is the roundtable discussion of our holy works.

I've been working to turn the consciousness of ECK toward being more open to service in the world, to carry the message of Light and Sound to the world in a way the world can understand. But this isn't easy. Oddly enough, my greatest opposition doesn't come from the community but actually from within the membership. People like to attach themselves to some point in the past when things felt good.

The ECK teachings must fit into a pattern that is somewhat parallel to the beliefs of people we are trying to reach. Sometimes when I give a talk, it comes out different from what I expected. My notes go in another direction. At times I'm like a bystander, watching it. It surprises me too, because I hadn't developed the thoughts in that direction. But the talk always turns out as it should to fit the spiritual needs of those listening.

Strawberry Shortcake

I sometimes go to a restaurant for carryout food when I'm in a hurry or working on a project at home. In one particular restaurant there's a bakery. I don't often eat sweets because they take a toll on my teeth, but this time as I waited for my food order, I passed the time by staring at the baked goods.

The glass case was filled with beautiful apple pies that stood four or five inches tall—with crusts like you wouldn't believe. Then I saw a strawberry shortcake. It was twice as tall as the apple pie!

When I came home I tried to describe that strawberry shortcake to my wife. But you just can't describe something like that. You have to experience it.

About two weeks later, my wife went to pick up carryout food at the same restaurant. When she came home, she said, "There was the most wonderful strawberry shortcake I've ever seen." Her eyes were all lit up. I said, "That's the one. You don't have to say another word about it, because now I know you know."

It's the same way with our spiritual realizations. They're better than strawberry shortcake when they come. They transform an individual's life.

Finding a Champion

One Higher Initiate discovered a very interesting principle: Before you can get any project done, you need a champion. Champions carry a project because their love is in it. You want to look for people like this; they'll probably know what needs to be done.

As we go further along in ECKANKAR, as history begins to unfold behind us, we're going to find that some initiates like to do just one thing, because that is where their heart is. They might feel more comfortable being teachers. Others will be in the works of love. Still others will be missionaries. Each area of service draws upon a different kind of strength.

Sometimes people have great enthusiasm but they're off track a little. Maybe they just need direction; they have a lot of enthusiasm for doing something, but it's not quite ECK. A little nudge can often adjust things without killing their spirit. You don't want to get heavy. In a nice, up-front manner you can say, "If you do it like this, then it will be all right."

When things grow fast in an area, it just means you're giving people a chance to serve. You're letting them do the things they want to do instead of what you decide they should or shouldn't do.

Some love Vahana work as a main endeavor. It is what makes ECKANKAR fun for them. Others like to be Arahatas because they like to see people unfold spiritually through the Satsang classes. The missionary finds the people, then the Arahata takes over from the missionary. The two areas work together.

Working Together

There was a story about four people: everybody, somebody, anybody, and nobody. An important job needed to be done, and everybody was asked to do it.

Everybody was sure somebody would do it. Anybody could have done it, but nobody did it. Somebody got angry about that because it was everybody's job. Everybody thought anybody could do it, but nobody realized that everybody wouldn't do it.

It ended up that everybody blamed somebody when

actually nobody asked anybody.

But I asked the RESAs. Essentially that's it. It takes someone at home to actually be a replica, in a limited form, of the Living ECK Master, so that there is somebody in charge.

Many years ago, I went into a Laundromat and wanted to put up an ECK poster. I got my papers laid down and my thumbtacks out, and I started to put up the poster. The man in charge of the Laundromat came out and asked me about it. "If it's any religious or political group," he said, "I don't want it." I didn't even try to explain ECK to him.

Then I went to put a notice in the newspaper. The woman behind the counter was quite formidable. She went to check on it, then she said no. I always felt uncomfortable with authority, so I said OK.

At that time I didn't have the courage to pursue either of these situations. There are many of us, as we put out the message of ECK, who don't have the courage. But what we have now are other ECKists, if we can just learn to work together.

The dream taught him that the time to take personal action was upon us.

5

Responsibilities of the Higher Initiate

A Higher Initiate wrote me about a dream. In the dream he attended a Higher Initiates' meeting on one of the inner planes. The group of H.I.'s expected me to talk, but instead I assigned everyone a project.

All of the Higher Initiates were to go out and find one personal project, task, or interest which they could accomplish or present to the public which would share the message of ECK.

The Higher Initiate said this was a surprise. He wrote, "It changed our roles from listeners to doers, which was exactly your purpose. Everyone dispersed for this task and returned a short time later for show-and-tell. It was a great success."

He said that the dream taught him that the time to take personal action was upon us.

Taking Personal Action

Sometimes all these extensive programs we develop take the heart out of the role of the Higher Initiate. That role is doing. Not doing just according to some outer direction, although we do have to keep in touch. It's doing inwardly.

In a similar vein, the ECK discourses have a number of spiritual exercises and techniques. We can get very involved in discussing them, but as Paul Twitchell once mentioned, "Why don't you just do it?" It's so simple.

As the right arm of the Mahanta, you have much to give those around you. They look to you. And as you serve, they study your every action. Sometimes you even have to be careful of the words you speak. You mean something as a joke, and someone else takes it seriously.

You also have to go slow, plan well, and not burn yourself out. It's better to work slowly and surely toward a goal than to put forth a great spurt of energy, then collapse—just when the initiates are finally warming up to you. Pick a pace that suits you, and stay with it.

How Your Life Affects the Whole

We must always keep before us the goal we're trying to reach. I'll admit keeping the ideal of God Consciousness before us is difficult when our daily lives seem less than exciting in our own eyes.

The things that occur sometimes seem so unnecessary. We wonder, *What am I doing in my profession, in my life? Is it going to matter at all to anyone in spiritual history when I'm gone?* The truth is that as one person is raised in spiritual consciousness, all are raised.

As in all things—whether it is something you're doing here on earth or in the spiritual worlds—you either go forward or you go backward. It may seem sometimes that you can rest, that you can go into a state of limbo. But during this state you're not totally at rest:

you're moving forward or you're moving backward. This is just the way the spiritual law works.

When Higher Initiates Leave ECK

Very often I have to overlook many of the things Higher Initiates do. These individuals are learning the laws of ECK. They're learning them in the only way that means something to them personally.

The ECK writings say that the Mahanta lets go of the initiate's hand at the Fifth Plane. What often happens is that the initiate lets go of the Mahanta's hand. If he does this, he'll wander around for a long time. Only the Mahanta, the Living ECK Master can bring Soul to the Eleventh Circle. So how does a person expect to get through the initiations past the Fifth alone?

When a Higher Initiate steps out of ECK, he stays in a certain time and space. The unfoldment of the circle of ECK initiates moves forward continually. Perhaps what was a Fifth Initiate four or five years ago is equivalent to a Fourth Initiate in ECK today.

If people leave ECK, I say, "You're welcome to go." Twenty or 30 percent of them will be back in a few years, because they need more experience. They may have gone too fast in ECK and didn't have the inner preparation.

Probably vanity or a lack of self-discipline got the upper hand, and they didn't do the spiritual exercises. This connection with the ECK and the Mahanta is absolutely essential.

We always give people the freedom to make up their own minds. The true teachings are not in any physical book. If you stop there, you're going to have the letter but not the spirit of the teachings; and you're going to be left behind.

Coming Home Again

I get letters from people who want to come back to ECKANKAR. They've lost something precious. Money and possessions have no meaning anymore because the love of the ECK and the Mahanta is gone. It just takes them a while to realize it.

Sometimes ECKists are surprised that I reinstate people at relatively high initiations. But I say, "Look at what they've learned." They've probably learned more than initiates who stayed in ECK and never had to fall after traveling so far up the mountain.

Compassion for Others

When we see others falling or stumbling, we are seeing our own ability to fall and stumble. So when people walk along the razor's edge and don't always do it well, we have to demonstrate some compassion and understanding. We expect compassion from others while we are learning about our relationship with the ECK, the Mahanta, and the SUGMAD. We ought to have the broadness of vision to allow others to stumble and grope and find their way back home to the highest realization.

If a Higher Initiate is out of balance, I sometimes let the situation run until other initiates become aware of the problem. They will then take this person aside and say, "You say you have this great consciousness, but your actions and behavior don't show it. How come?" It's better if the chelas themselves tell a person he's out of balance rather than my having to do it.

After the period of imbalance comes the time of trouble. Then comes the time of tears and the feeling of separation, where a person asks, "Why has the Master forsaken me?" Give compassion when this happens, because if the time ever comes when you are out of balance, you'll need compassion more than ever.

Rest Points

When a person steps off the path to rest, he goes backward. This is because the spiral of consciousness goes ever upward. The ECK is always expanding. Even when people think they're standing still, they are either moving with the ECK and expanding or they are moving backward.

I've set a five-year limit. Within that time period a person, at my discretion, can come back at the level of initiation he left. Sometimes I may require him to spend up to a year in the previous initiation or previous two initiations before I let him reenter the higher circles. He has to be in harmony with the other Higher Initiates of today.

Being Kind to Yourself

One of the definitions of *Co-workers with God* is "partners with God" or "partners with life." This involves, first of all, learning to be kind to ourselves as individuals.

Even with the Friday fast, there are three levels of fasting. If a person has a health problem, I would not suggest the Friday water fast. By going without food, some people spiritually harm themselves more than if they eat something on Friday.

When I was young, my body could make up the difference and take on some of the shock. I wouldn't be able to do the water fast today because I'm older. So I don't expect people to forget their common sense when it comes to the Friday fasts.

There are two other kinds of fast that may fit you better: the partial food fast or the juice fast, and the mental fast. The latter is keeping your attention upon the Mahanta, the ECK, or the SUGMAD—or all three, because there really is no difference in the spiritual sense. In a human sense there is, but that is the mind trying to make divisions so it can understand something that is not within the scope of human understanding.

Staying Sensible

True ECKists are going to be very sensible people in everyday life. They're not going to be half strung out. They're going to have some control over their tempers. I know sometimes when you're at work, it's not easy. But that's what life is for—to test you, to take you to the very edge of your patience, and to teach you. As long as we're on earth, we fight with the five passions of the mind.

Some feel that as soon as they get to the Fifth Plane all karma is gone, that they work without karma. This is the ideal Paul Twitchell set up for Higher Initiates in *The Shariyat*. But we find that people are people, and everyone has a unique state of consciousness. That state is not fixed; it changes because the forces of the lower worlds play upon the individual.

You might say that the spiritual state of consciousness is above the material planes and should not be affected in any way. That's true, it shouldn't. But there

46

is a balance between the inner and the outer worlds. A person's outer state is dictated by his inner state, which is often not as great as the individual thinks it is.

Overcoming Alcoholism

One Higher Initiate told me this story. He had a problem with drinking. It was interfering with his spiritual progress, and he decided to go cold turkey. For a month he had the shakes, just like an ordinary street wino in the drunk tank.

After he came out of the withdrawal period, he felt pretty good. He felt he was over it. Shortly thereafter he had an inner experience.

Shamus-i-Tabriz came to him in a kitchen. On the kitchen floor was a large crate which Shamus opened. Inside were twelve big bottles of the very finest wine.

Shamus told the Higher Initiate, "Each one of these bottles is from a different ECK Master, and each bottle comes from the time that ECK Master served as the Mahanta on earth. The wine is from many ages, and it represents the very best there is."

"Well, if you'll excuse me, I've given up drinking," said the Higher Initiate. Shamus said, "This is a gift of the Vairagi. You will drink it." And Shamus stood there and watched while the Higher Initiate drank the first bottle.

The Higher Initiate finally lost consciousness, and when he awoke, he was in a room of blinding white light. If you've ever had a hangover, you know that your head feels like it's splitting open anyway, without the extra encouragement of blinding white light.

This room of bright light happened to be in the belfry of a Golden Wisdom Temple, and the man's head

47

was underneath a huge golden bell. Immediately the bell began to ring, and the man thought his head would come off. He lost consciousness again.

He awoke on a beach and walked off his drunken stupor. When it was over, Shamus-i-Tabriz took him back to the kitchen and said, "Now drink the second bottle."

Taking Responsibility

Alcoholism is not a worse passion of the mind than any of the others, but it's a behavior pattern that can cause you many problems. If you have a need for alcohol and you haven't overcome it, don't bring evidence of your intoxication in front of other chelas. It could make them stumble on the path to God. If this happens, then I have to discipline you.

During Paul Twitchell's time, some Higher Initiates had problems with drinking, but no one knew it. They were able to keep their need for alcohol in check, at least during an ECK seminar. I feel bad when I hear of Higher Initiates breaking for the bar as soon as the evening talk is over.

In the past I have given the initiations relatively quickly up to certain levels, but I am slowing them down. People who have problems with drinking, in certain cases, won't be permitted to go further. If their behavior becomes a problem in Satsang class, I may even have to remove some of their responsibilities. I cannot have an Initiator giving an initiation reeking of alcohol. I take the ECK initiations and the ESA sessions very seriously.

I can't tell you how to work if you are in a position of ECK leadership. Sometimes those who work with me in the office will, but generally I try not to. There's a reason for it. When I have to take it upon myself to talk to someone and tell them that their actions are harming others spiritually, this often does more damage to the Higher Initiate.

Maintaining Individuality

More important than the information you give others as a Higher Initiate is sharing your own experiences with them. For example, in Satsang class, choose the main idea from the discourse lesson and ask the different chelas in class, "What about this discourse seems most important to you?" Then speak about your own experience, from the heart.

Encourage the students to challenge your viewpoint—"Is this what you saw? You may not see it the way I've seen it." This melts the inner iceberg. The Satsang class is really a process of spiritual transformation which does not depend upon the written word in the discourse. You're not doing the transforming; the ECK is.

Marriage is basically the individual's effort to find balance within himself. Out here we try to find it with another human being.

6

Families and Relationships

There isn't a stronger bond than family. As we get to know each other, we become better vehicles for the divine ECK.

When a person looks for a marriage partner, he looks for something to complement himself. If he has strong outgoing tendencies, he may find someone who's not so outgoing. Together they make the perfect balance as a couple. You can call these positive or negative traits, but it's really a stronger or lesser trait in a certain direction.

Marriage is basically the individual's effort to find balance within himself. Out here we try to find it with another human being.

Being Spiritually Considerate

In relationships, we must be spiritually considerate of others' strengths and weaknesses. Although we really don't have secrets as H.I.'s, people who come to an H.I. meeting and think it is dull maybe aren't considering the energy that's flowing there. It speeds things up in your relationship. It could unbalance it.

It could cause problems in a family if a spouse came to the meeting before becoming an H.I. The problems that would come up are not easily traced back to the meeting. It'll look like something mundane: the kitchen sink wasn't wiped off. But there could be more and more anger in the relationship.

People don't understand that the initiate who came to the meeting got burned by too much ECK flow. The individual didn't have the transforming power built in as protection yet.

The Power of ECK

The ECK is a force and power that most people don't understand. It grows stronger with each initiation. When a Higher Initiate reaches another level or we turn a few more Fifths loose in the world, it has an effect.

At one seminar I invited six people to my hotel room to give them the next higher initiation. I went to the bathroom before anyone arrived and flushed the toilet. I noticed the water was running very fast, so I jiggled the handle. The top of the toilet flew off. There must have been ninety pounds of pressure in the pipes.

It was directly tied to the initiations. If you do too much, things break. You have to regulate the flow a little bit.

Self-Responsibility

When something good happens on the inner, we like to take credit, but when something bad happens, we like to blame someone else. Ultimately you are responsible for everything that happens in your own inner worlds. There's never anyone outside yourself in your own world. The forms that exist there are the ones you allow out of your imagination.

Sometimes the inner changes are the most difficult. The outer things are just outer things; they're not as important as how you react to them. That's what's important.

Respect for Each Other

You may disagree with your loved ones, but you have to have respect for each other. If you don't have respect, you don't have a family.

Listening to each other is very important. When listening breaks down in a family, the marriage partners drift farther and farther apart.

As soon as we learn to listen, the ECK flow opens, and we become more successful in our relationships.

Making the Way Better

Higher Initiates sometimes look at the delays in life as misfortunes. You assume that if you hadn't been delayed, everything would have gone fine, without any stress or strain. But think about what might have happened if you had gone on with your original plans in other situations. You wouldn't be here today.

As we move through life, the ECK steps in to make our way better. With the limited viewpoint of the human consciousness, we put our attention on the delays instead of the blessings. Because we do this, we often become angry or upset with family or loved ones.

Healing Spiritual Shortages

We tend to become upset when there's a shortage of something. For instance, if we're short on time, we let everyone around us know we are very busy, important people and we have to get going. The message is Please get out of my way.

Perhaps if we looked at ourselves a little more carefully, we'd find the shortage came because we failed to plan enough. Often because we don't plan, we are angry and bitter. And we end up pointing fingers at someone else for the problems in our own lives.

We find it even harder to accept self-responsibility for our money shortages. There's either enough or there's not. The person who has enough is usually someone else.

With our vision on the shortages—because we have failed to plan to make our lives better—we forget the blessings. We overlook them. It happens to all of us when we forget that the ECK is working in our lives every minute for our good. All we have to do is recognize it.

How do we recognize it? Usually with the Spiritual Exercises of ECK.

The Real Reason for the Spiritual Exercises

Often when I talk about the Spiritual Exercises of ECK, people say, "He's talking about duty." Duty means an extra burden, something that takes time which we don't have because we are too busy with more important things. We don't have time to let Spirit come into our lives and help us plan. So we end up with shortages.

It's a lack of discipline. Lack of discipline comes through lack of spiritual understanding. That's why I say, "Do your spiritual exercises." Because in doing them you allow the Holy Spirit, or the ECK, to come into your lives. Then you are able to plan better because you are getting divine guidance. It makes a lot of difference.

The wisdom you're looking for is in the Spiritual Exercises of ECK. If you have spiritual shortages, at least make enough time for the spiritual exercises.

Unless we have quality in a spiritual sense at the very core of our being, we won't have the strength needed to survive.

7

Moving through the Higher Initiations

When an individual comes to the Fifth Plane, he is already preparing to enter into the first levels of the Ninth Initiation. On the higher planes, there is no clear, structured delineation where one plane leaves off and the next one begins. They flow together, blending like different colors on an artist's palette.

The higher you go, the tighter the requirements are, and the more discriminating I become. Second Initiations are pretty much for anybody who asks. For the Third and Fourth, the requirements get a little strict. By the time a person reaches the Fifth Circle, it's pretty tight. It gets tighter yet for the Sixth.

Steps in the Higher Initiations

The initiate of the Sixth Circle has become well-grounded in the basic laws of Spirit. His life may not outwardly settle down, but he settles down inside. He has more spiritual strength to roll with the punches, to understand and accommodate the changes coming into his life.

The Sixth is more or less a refined, higher Fifth

Initiation. The person has come to understand the spiritual laws of the Soul Plane quite well. He is moving on, laying the groundwork for becoming a Seventh Initiate.

The Seventh Initiation is quite a transition from the Sixth. Between the Sixth and the Seventh quite a change occurs both inwardly and outwardly. There's a greater move between the Sixth and the Seventh than between the Fifth and the Sixth.

The Eighth Initiation allows much more freedom than Soul experienced in the Seventh. While the initiate is enjoying this freedom, he is able to work more or less in full consciousness with the Vairagi Masters. He is about to enter the first of the initiatory circles of the Vairagi Order, the neophyte level of the ECK Adepts which begins at the Ninth Plane.

When a person gets to be a Ninth Initiate, the initiation is given quietly on the inner. By this time it should be obvious to God and man that the person has made it past the Eighth. Even at the Eighth and the Ninth, you have to watch carefully. If you're still here, it means there are still things you are learning.

A Second Initiate may enjoy a higher state of consciousness sometimes than even an Eighth. It just depends upon what that Eighth Initiate's experience is at the moment. If his mind has been running in a circle, he'll probably be unhappy and will not be in the highest state of awareness. The Second Initiate will breeze right by in a state of consciousness.

How Fast Are You Moving?

Anyone with an initiation in ECK is in the inner circle, the inner organization. Provisions are being made for people who touch ECK now so that in a future lifetime they can be in the same envious spiritual position you are in today.

Some of the early initiates in ECK put in their time during previous lives. They were able to move into the Higher Initiations very quickly today. We're making this possible for those in the future. Global communications exist today for the spiritual purpose of bringing the message of ECK to the world.

The new people are very much ahead of what we were when we came in years ago. Some Higher Initiates who are not active tell me they want to come back in at their original initiation level as a Seventh. But at this point they are barely a Fourth. That's the nature of the upliftment of consciousness, the expansion which occurs.

Life Is Change

Life isn't just touched with change; life is change. You can't resist change; it is part of life. Change constantly works in your life whether you like it or not, whether you agree with it or not. Change is going on constantly because life is going on constantly.

The more you want to live in the past and recapture a lost childhood, the more difficult it is to be happy inside yourself. If you are lodged too deeply in the past, you find that you can't be happy today. It's like visiting a place where you once lived as a child. Years later, when you go back to visit, somehow there's a feeling of sadness.

The past is the past. And the present is ever changing to bring us to tomorrow.

Surrender Brings Smoothness

Some Higher Initiates tell people who come into ECKANKAR that when you get on this path, it gets really hard. They lay this trip on them. Not everybody has it hard. A lot of us can have it fairly easy. It depends on how quickly we can surrender to Spirit.

If the ECK is coming into a person strongly, he can't help being out among people, serving in some way. Some of it's going to show; he can't keep it all to himself.

From Human to God Consciousness

Some people say, "I am in the human state of consciousness today, and tomorrow I'll be God-Realized." But in making this jump to what they imagine God-Realization to be, they make a false jump. They jump into a condition that is neither spiritual nor helpful to anyone. When they declare themselves God-Realized, either directly or by suggestion, they are simply looking to gather followers.

To them, God-Realization equals having followers. They get so interested in gathering followers—at whatever cost to themselves or others—that they forget about living life. They forget about the purpose of living life.

I put attention not on the state of God-Realization but on the process—the day-to-day living. Because God-Realization is not a state where one becomes self-serving, but where one serves others.

There isn't any hurry with the initiations. I want to make sure that the initiates who come into ECK and move into the higher initiations are good ones. There are always going to be those who were good when they came in but somewhere they faltered. And there are those who got in just by the skin of their teeth and they got stronger.

Unless we have quality in a spiritual sense at the very core of our being, we won't have the strength needed to survive.

The dog ran thirty feet right straight up the trunk of that tree. Not because he could, but because he had to.

8

Spiritual Problem Solving

There was an article in *Natural History* magazine by Roger Welsch called "Dry Humor." Welsch was talking to an old-timer about the drought in the 1930s, about all the hardships that happened—the bank failures, fires, floods, farm accidents.

Welsch said the old man reported that his "hogs dried out so bad during the thirties that the critters would get cracks between their ribs. He had to soak them in the creek just so they would hold a slop." He added that one day he went with his dad to dig a well. When they found water, they were happy until they tested it for moisture content and found it only had 37 percent.

Welsch knew the old-timer was really stretching it, so he asked the man, "How is it that you can tell me such funny stories at the same time you're telling me about a life that sounds like nothing but tragedy?"

The old-timer said, "I'm not an educated man, so I can't tell you the psychology or the philosophy of the matter . . . but I can tell you another story." So he told a story about a hunting trip to the river bottom.

His dog had come up against a bobcat. Bobcats like to eat dogs for lunch. They're particularly ferocious animals. The bobcat took off after the dog and was gaining on it. Down in the river bottom were big cotton-woods. The old-timer said the dog "ran thirty feet right straight up the trunk of that tree. . . . That dog didn't climb the tree because he could; he climbed it because he *had* to."

The article showed that, when times are hard, you do things out of necessity. You also learn to laugh. There's nothing else you can do.

Solving Very Basic Problems

When I travel and stay in hotels, I often shred my confidential work and flush it down the toilet. I have letters that I don't want the hotel people to see. I had quite a pile one day, so I filled the toilet and flushed. But the toilet got clogged, and the paper wouldn't go down.

The evening got later, and I kept working, throwing more shredded paper into the toilet. The water came right up to the rim of the toilet bowl, then gradually went down. "Maybe some great wizard will come while I'm asleep and fix this," I said. "When I wake up in the morning, it will be completely fixed." I woke up at 2:00 a.m., and I knew it wasn't fixed.

It was that time of the morning when I couldn't call the front desk and say, "Please send someone to fix my toilet." The maintenance man would come in, see the toilet filled with paper, and say, "Fool." And since I would be too tired to think of witty things to say, I'd just sit there. This kind of interaction would haunt me for the entire weekend. So I thought I'd try to fix it myself.

I found a hotel utility bag in the closet. I blew air into it. Then I tied knots in it to make smaller sections, to make a sort of plumber's helper. I even came up with several intricate designs. I plunged it into the bowl and worked it up and down carefully, trying not to burst it. And the clogged toilet suddenly cleared. I flushed it once, twice, three times, saying to myself, I did it!

Sometimes we get too far from the basics of life. Whenever we get that far, that's probably when we deserve to be *in* the very basics of life. That's when we learn something.

If you succeed in solving the little things, it gives you the confidence to try something bigger.

Karmic Workout

As you unfold, you find you don't have fewer problems. This is true whether it's the individual or a group sitting around a table.

Your day-to-day karma could be gone, but the deep-seated things that keep you on earth boil up to be worked off. In your health, these deep-seated problems that are underneath come up in the form of sickness. You're changing the vibration of the body as you unfold.

Learn to work with your inner state. For instance, let's say you have a dream or some kind of an experience which lines up a certain number of events. In your dream you see something happening which you would not want to happen. Usually at this point I get letters from people who say, "I'm having nightmares; can you please stop them? I don't want any more."

Very seldom do these initiates ask me to show them how to help themselves.

When these inner events come up, you just need to change one or more of the elements. This way you can help yourself. For instance, in a dream you see yourself walking down a particular street. It's dark outside, and you see several people lying in wait in an alley. They are going to attack you. (These dreams can be a lot subtler than I've mentioned here too.) What can you do?

For one thing, don't walk down the alley. Or you can go with someone else. In other words, if you have a dream of warning, change some of the elements out here in the physical.

If you're on the path of ECK, there are times when you will go into the other worlds and face terrifying things you'd rather not see. It's part of the spiritual education. You can never test your spiritual strength and get stronger if everything is going right all the time.

Routines

Our habits and mental activity usually run in a routine. Because we run in a routine, we have certain ways of doing things and approaching problems. Going about our lives, we invite certain things to happen to us. If the Inner Master gives us an insight into what's about to come, it doesn't mean it's inevitable. It means that if we have any smarts, we can choose to do something to change the future.

You change the future by changing one, two, or more elements. In other words, you're changing your routine. You're changing the normal arrangement of your mental patterns. This can lead to the expansion of consciousness—when you're revising and going beyond the box of the mind.

It's all right to make a plan, but it's also OK to change plans. In fact, in ECK you're going to find that once you set up a good, basic plan for something you're going to have to change many of the little details to make it work properly. Things come up that you haven't foreseen, even when you think everything has been taken care of.

The Master tries to give you the benefit of your own past experience, which is also colored by routines established in the past. They have led us to the experiences we have had so far.

The Master will give you an inner experience. He'll say, "Here's something that's coming up." What he doesn't say is that it's because of a routine. It's the result of your mechanical mode of action. If you will exercise the creative power of Soul and do something different, you can change your future.

This is the single thing that should set you apart from a person who is in the beginning stages of the ECK initiations. You ought to become aware of your inner states. It is here that the Master is telling you, not once but two or three times, to exercise caution in a certain area and how to go about it.

Your Inner Creations

Nightmares can be good because they show an impurity in the spiritual state of the individual. But most people ask me to take away the nightmares instead of asking me how to understand and work with their own inner creations.

Those who have problems like nightmares are often having problems functioning on the outer. Lack of confidence is often the gentlest problem they have. People are often very imbalanced in a number of ways.

I'm the spiritual mirror of your experiences. I realize that when it's difficult on my end, it's very likely

67

difficult on your end. These are times when you must almost desperately fix your attention on the Mahanta; there's nothing else that'll pull you through a time like this.

Recognizing Real Protection

People expect to have no troubles. They ask, "Why didn't the Master protect me?" But the purpose of life isn't to live without problems. The Master is interested in the expansion of consciousness so that each one of you may reach God-Realization one day.

As soon as you can accept the works of ECK with at least some degree of openness, then you can have the spiritual protection of the Master. But life keeps giving you problems—even if you're a Higher Initiate, even if you're under the protection of the Master. People who don't understand the spiritual works might say, "That's not protection, because everything isn't being done for me." But they're so wrong.

This is part of the fallacy of the orthodox teachings. As ECKists, we have to put these false beliefs aside. The teaching of truth brings a true understanding of what the protection of the Master means. It doesn't take away all your self-responsibility; it actually puts more on you.

Spiritual Arrogance

You may expect to come to the top of the mountain and say, "Here I am; so what now?" That's not how life goes. Life goes up and down. I had to go up the mountain, then come down the other side, back to everyday living. That's the challenge we must face.

68

When a human being gets something too fast and too easily, he finds it a treasure of almost no value. He becomes arrogant.

When the trials come, he doesn't recognize them as trials. When a test of faith comes, he doesn't recognize it as a test of faith. He judges everything according to the human consciousness, either right or wrong.

When people become arrogant with something as powerful as the ECK teachings, they burn out spiritually. That's why so few of the early ECK initiates who were given their initiations quickly have survived in ECKANKAR today.

Necessary Resistance

Sometimes we find it very difficult to get out of bed in the morning. Why do we feel so heavy? Maybe our physical bodies are having a difficult bout with gravity. But if we didn't have gravity—or resistance in disguise—we would become so weak that we couldn't walk. Resistance and trouble are necessary.

If we wish to become partners, or Co-workers, with God, we must learn to accept resistance and learn how to work with it. Sometimes this resistance may come from our enemies and sometimes from our friends. But there's a way to make it work. This way is found by practicing divine love. Find ways to live divine love.

The HU Chant is an opportunity for people to come together in a group and experience the Audible Life Current. This is everything that ECK is about: to experience the Sound and Light of God in whatever way we can, whenever we can.

9

Light and Sound Experiences

When I went to Africa in 1983 or 1984, there was a gentleman there who whistled beautifully. He just stood onstage, threw back his shoulders, and began to whistle his love song to God.

Sound is so important to us all, but to the Africans it's especially vital. I wish you could hear them chant. It's part of their culture; they chant so well, and they sing so beautifully.

The HU Chant is an opportunity for people to come together in a group and experience the Audible Life Current. This is everything that ECK is about: to experience the Sound and Light of God in whatever way we can, whenever we can.

The Spiritual Purpose of HU Chants

Some Higher Initiates ask me about HU Chants. They wonder if it's OK for people to come to the chant, sing HU just a few times, then sit in silence absorbing the sound. Is this the kind of HU Chant we're looking for? they wonder.

In the HU Chant, you have to give. You give by chanting. I don't have a great voice, but I get by. I chant more quietly than those with beautiful voices. You can make the connection with the Light and Sound even with a voice like mine.

Is it necessary to chant out loud? I'd say it's better, because you are giving instead of just receiving the energies of the ECK.

This is the purpose of the HU Chant, because there is a power in group chanting that can inspire and uplift a person. The Light is important, but the Sound is more important.

An Inner Pace

A woman was talking with her spouse about the Light and Sound. She really didn't remember hearing or seeing anything, and she asked if he did. He was hearing one of the sounds, but he said, "It's always the same sound; sometimes it's just louder."

Many initiates have forgotten or aren't sure what they inwardly hear or see. Some, like the woman's husband, take it for granted; it's just part of them. The Sound Current actually gives this ECKist the motion to live and have his being. He's moving to an inner pace.

Some people may look at him and say he moves too slow. He has a measured pace; yet if you don't try and push him, he gets along fine.

Do We Really Have Inner Experiences?

Often we feel we aren't having inner experiences. Then we begin to wonder if anyone else is really having them.

In our instant society, we're used to things being done quickly. Some people have inner experiences very easily; for others it can take ten or fifteen years before one comes along that they recognize. If there are resistances within a person and he were put into the other worlds before he was ready, there would be more harm done than good.

The students of ECK have experiences with the Holy Spirit that are stronger and clearer than in any other religious organization on earth. This is what makes ECKANKAR precious. That's why I'm not too concerned about the outer form that ECKANKAR has to take to survive.

All I care about is that there is a conductor for the Light and Sound to come into the world. There are many Souls waiting to find their way back home to God.

Working in Other Dimensions

Most people would limit the ability of Soul to see, know, and be everywhere at one and the same time. They limit It to one body at a time.

Those of you who are able to remember your inner experiences may find you'll be in places you would think you've never been before. Yet night after night you'll go to different places, and it feels like you've been there before.

This is because you already have an identity established in that place. There are people who know you on the inner planes and who rely on you. You've made commitments to them, and they've made commitments to you. In other words, you are living a life on the other planes at different levels.

After you get into the higher states of consciousness

and you are able to remember your experiences on other planes, you'll find that the mind can only bring back a little bit of what you've experienced. You'll have different experiences, but you'll know you've been there before and you know these people. You don't know them here, but you know them there.

Soul can be in many places at the same time. It can occupy many bodies in many different universes at the same time. You're serving SUGMAD in such a wide range of existence. I search for words sometimes, trying to do justice to the majesty of Soul. It's the ability to see, know, and be.

Remembering What Happened

I'm interested in you remembering your inner experiences. Not everybody is able to do this. I want you to have the assurance and confidence to work with the ECK initiates. They can tell whether or not you know if ECK is true and real. They can feel it by just being around you.

Why do we forget our experiences? Many times what happens is very much in harmony with what we understand outwardly. Therefore there is no ripple. Our senses are only activated by ripples of some sort.

When you move into a new area, you'll remember things very clearly at first, probably for a week or month or two. Then you get used to the plane and it seems natural.

So many Higher Initiates still haven't had what we'd call classic Soul Travel experiences—where they go zooming out of the body or have the expansion of consciousness and know without a doubt that this is Soul Travel. If we heard the Sound and saw the Light at all times in Its full glory, It would blind us to what had to be done in this physical plane.

Soul Travel is a lower-world phenomenon. It's enjoyable for a time, but like other things, you give it up. In the Higher Initiations, it's important to know that you don't have to try so hard to do Soul Travel.

As you work more directly with the Light and Sound, you ought to be able to move into the other worlds in full consciousness. Maybe not initially, where you're conscious of moving into the other worlds in full awareness, but being aware of the other worlds, working with other people, being a Co-worker with the Mahanta.

The Eye of God

An ECKist had an experience where she saw the single Eye of God. It was just a big eye hanging in the heavens. This always means the single-minded striving toward the state of God-Realization.

Then three eagle feathers floated down from the sky. She wondered what it meant. It was simply an indication of those who are flying high in the sky, trying to reach the sun: The feathers were the only thing we could see down here. No matter what initiation we're in, we can fly high in our own worlds.

Perfection in Soul

The spiritual exercises are given for us to find perfection as Soul. They will teach us the self-discipline we need to serve God.

When you do the spiritual exercises, you may wonder what is going to happen. There were times I was afraid, and just like that I would snap back from an experience. All I can say is, Love the ECK so much that you don't care what happens.

I try to provide a number of different spiritual exercises. It gives you the idea that you can create one yourself. Ultimately I am trying to get you to do this. Find your own spiritual exercise for each particular time. As you go along, you're naturally going to use different ones. It's part of the unfolding process.

ECK-Vidya Experiences

Some of you have special gifts, such as being shown through the ECK-Vidya what is to come. Fourteen years before it was built, a Higher Initiate had an experience of flying over the site of the ECK Temple in Chanhassen, Minnesota. This is seeing the future through the ECK-Vidya.

Some ECKists think I'm making everything up as we go along. But it's already in the works. If this Higher Initiate had just imagined her experience, she certainly wouldn't have seen a frozen lake. She might have seen a nice blue lake in Florida or Australia, but certainly not a wintry landscape covered with ice and snow. What she was seeing was already established on the inner planes, ready to manifest out here.

Even though a person is a Fifth Initiate and established on the Soul Plane, he'll sometimes miss out on the high realizations because he doesn't keep up with the spiritual exercises.

Changes in Consciousness

It's a funny thing with consciousness. When you lose it, you're not conscious of having lost it.

People who are on the borderline in ECK watch Higher Initiates who've left ECK. They say, "Hey, they're just as bright as anyone in ECK. They're doing OK. There's nothing wrong with them. They have the same level of consciousness they had before!" But they don't. Two people of the same cloth are judging each other, seeing in each other old-time friends of the same stature.

People who leave ECK lose some Light and Sound. All people have Light and Sound, but they don't have It to the degree that ECKists have as an overall rule.

Have you ever seen kittens chase their tails? One day they notice this thing flying around behind them. They've never seen it before, and it's their own tail. So they start chasing it, and they go round and round, totally happy. Once in a while, they bite their tails and cry, "Ouch!"

People who leave ECK run in a tight circle like kittens chasing their tails. They'll probably be chasing their tails, going nowhere, until they're just lucky enough to catch the tail, bite it, and have a shock of pain. This is usually life biting them. And suddenly they catch on.

That's the return to consciousness. The channel inside them opens again, and the Light and Sound begin to come in, very slowly. This is when I get letters from people who've left two, three, four years ago. They realize their life is dead; the Light's gone out. The Light is gone, the Sound is gone. And they ask me, "Can I come back?"

The opportunity came to this particular ESA who had been feeling insecure about her abilities. After this experience, she knew that a greater love was at work during this sacred rite than her own.

10

Initiator and ECK Spiritual Aide

A staff member at the ECK office moved to Hawaii. Since she was tired of office work, she decided that her next job would be different. So she interviewed for a job selling jewelry in one of the shopping malls.

She was an ideal salesperson because she didn't try to sell anything to anybody. She just listened to them. She found that people usually told her exactly what they wanted. If they mentioned something, she took the next step. They'd say, "I'm looking for something like this." And she'd say, "You mean sort of like this?" and show them something.

Sometimes she'd go all day without making a sale; other times she'd sell fifteen thousand dollars' worth of jewelry in forty-five minutes. Her employer couldn't believe how much jewelry she sold.

Her example is important for Higher Initiates working as ECK Spiritual Aides (ESA). It's important to just listen to the people who come to you. Sometimes they will solve their own problems.

Give-and-Take

People who bring you their problems also bring their own answers. All you have to do is listen. If you let the ECK guide you, you're going to find being an ESA very easy.

When the person has a hard time talking about their problem because it is so close to them, they can't always state it right the first time. You can guide them a little here and there, maybe by repeating what they have told you.

You may restate things, but you can't give people answers to their problems. You can guide them to government offices for social help or assistance with very severe family problems. You can recommend counseling by professionals if they need that.

In this give-and-take that occurs in an ESA session, the ECK is bringing inner healing. It has nothing to do with you, per se, but it does—because you're an instrument for the ECK. And often you are the best instrument when you listen. It's actually the easiest thing of all to do.

Using Your Talents

Each of us have different talents. We develop those that are good for us. There is always plenty of work for each of us in every capacity, because we are so diverse in our abilities.

For example, not everyone has the talent to interpret inner experiences. Some people are very good at it; they like to do it. Others don't have any interest in doing it because they don't remember their own experiences.

Because of this, not everyone becomes an ECK Spiritual Aide. There simply isn't a need. I like to have people filling jobs for which there is a need. If there isn't a need, I would rather have Higher Initiates going into the community and doing whatever they can to present ECK in their own quiet way by being themselves.

Why Soul Is Here

ECKANKAR and the ECK teachings are so important, because through the experiences we have, the fear of death goes away. You can't live life fully until the fear of death is removed.

We're here for experience. We're not here to have things go perfectly, like in a utopia. That's not what Soul came here for.

Spiritual Qualifications

One of the Higher Initiates wrote me about her inadequacies as an ECK Spiritual Aide. She said she simply wondered if she had it within her to be an effective ESA, knowing herself as she did. I assured her that indeed she did have the spiritual qualifications to perform the service of spiritual listening for other people.

A short time after she got my letter, she was asked to do an initiation for an AIDS patient. Since he was on his deathbed, it turned out to be more than just an initiation. She had to use her spiritual insight as an ESA to complete the initiation.

The AIDS patient had had the pink slip for his Third Initiation for two years; by one circumstance or another, no Initiator was able to give him the initiation. Finally it came to the RESA's attention. She asked this ESA to give the initiation.

The man looked like a skeleton; he was so weak he could barely open his eyes. But he received his word and got his initiation. The ESA gave the blessings of the Mahanta in parting, and just an hour later the man translated.

The ESA wondered why none of the Initiators who had been approached were able to give the initiation. The real reason was that this ESA needed the experience. She had the exact spiritual understanding to fit that moment, and only she could gain the full benefit from this initiation.

Times change, and we often find ourselves in difficult situations, especially with something like AIDS. I can't tell any of you whether or not to give an initiation. You have to go to the Inner Master and find out for yourselves. If you're not the right person to do it, the Mahanta will not allow you to do it.

The opportunity came to this particular ESA who had been feeling insecure about her abilities. After this experience, she knew that a greater love was at work during this sacred rite than her own.

Rooted in the Earth

Our bodies are like cars, vans, or trucks. If your car broke down, how many of you would leave it parked on the freeway and go into contemplation to ask the Mahanta to make it run, expecting this to actually happen? The physical body is the same way.

If there's a physical or emotional problem, I recommend going to a medical doctor, a dentist, a psychotherapist, or a counselor. These are all means the ECK uses to give healing and peace of mind to all of you who need it. Avail yourselves of these things.

If someone is having problems with temper or drinking, it's OK to suggest that they seek professional counseling rather than saying, "Get help on the inner. The Mahanta will give it to you." Encourage people to seek professional help if you find that an ESA session or just talking with you as a Higher Initiate is not sufficient.

We are on the spiritual path, but our feet have to be firmly rooted in the earth. Earth is a spiritual training ground. It's not just a place to leave as quickly as possible, to get to the higher, pure regions. You'll never get to the higher, pure regions unless you have your full experience on earth.

Doorways into ECK

What if a person is making a living as a psychic healer, as an astrologer, or in one of the lower psychic arts? Often this is a doorway into ECK. Maybe people will find their way to ECK through this person.

A psychic healer was ready for his next initiation. The Higher Initiates in the area were reluctant to give him an endorsement for the Third Initiation. But I recommended that this person have another initiation, and I sent the pink slip out. Sometimes the person has to go just a little farther. I'd probably stop him at the Fourth Plane; I wouldn't let someone go into the Fifth Initiation who was still practicing as a psychic healer.

If a person is pulling people down from the high path of ECK into the lower psychic arts, I would have an objection. It's a problem when the traffic is going the wrong way. But it's generally OK if people are working quietly in these fields.

For example, a woman wrote me who wanted to be an auditor for Scientology. This involved helping certain people become clear. She felt this was a step on the spiritual path, which indeed it is. So I asked her just to work quietly. She is not to lead ECKists to Scientology, because that's not what we're about—to lead people to other paths. But if there are some in Scientology who become interested in what she thinks about life and want to know more about ECK, she can tell them.

In one area an H.I. got involved in another group then began promoting it to other chelas. This was wrong-way traffic on the path of ECK, leading people away from ECK. You're the doorway for traffic toward the SUGMAD. When you're the doorway toward the Kal, you're not acting in your capacity as a Higher Initiate.

Gauging Initiation Eligibility

An ECK chela asked me if all the ECK initiations were arranged by computer. He wanted to know if somewhere there was a human being that got involved. I said, "Frankly, I get involved."

One of the main ways initiation recommendations come to me is through the computer. If a person has put in the required study time for any initiation level, once or twice a year the computer coughs up the name.

Then I ask, Is this person an example of what an ECKist should be? From outer appearances, does he have evidence of Light and Sound in his life? This, of course, means a balanced individual. If you have the Light and Sound in your life, you have to be a balanced individual out here.

If I ask you for an initiation recommendation, give it as honestly as you can. Go into contemplation and say, "Make me a clear vehicle for the Mahanta." Don't recommend someone just because they're a friend or a relative.

If you can't recommend someone when you're asked, just simply say so, whatever the reason. You may not want to give a reason on paper, but if Spiritual Services calls up later and has a specific question, you may want to respond to it then.

If you feel the person is not deserving of the initiation, just say no. If it's for a spiritual reason based on *outer behavior*, it would help to note the fact: "Disrupts Satsang class. Does not listen to the directives of the RESA," and things like that.

If I ask you to make a recommendation for someone but you've never heard of the individual because they choose to live quietly, feel free to just say, "Unknown."

Please don't invade the person's privacy; if he has chosen to be private because that is a spiritual need, we should respect it. I have other ways of checking into a person's eligibility for another initiation.

Sometimes you may come upon someone who you feel is overdue for an initiation. Higher Initiates can forward the names to the RESA in the area, and I'll consider these people. We'll see if their study record is adequate; we'll check the records to find out if a person is qualified and ready.

In remote areas of the world where there is a need to put someone in a higher initiation, I may give an individual an initiation early. Likewise with someone who has served in an exceptional way. This is almost beyond understanding, but I will occasionally give an initiation sooner than the usual waiting time.

Sound Current

A new Initiator was asked to give an initiation at a seminar. Since no initiation rooms were available, someone suggested getting in a car, driving to the far end of the parking lot where it was quiet, and giving the initiation there. The Initiator was nervous but trying hard not to show it as she suggested the idea to the chela.

As soon as they started the initiation, a train whistle began blowing in the distance. It went wild. The new Initiator said it was just uncanny, and she mentioned it to another Initiator after the initiation.

The second Initiator said, "You'd be surprised how often the Sound will begin to pound on the initiation room. Sometimes you hear cars out in the street, honking and honking. Or it seems that a station wagon with steel wheels, no springs, and a load of lumber comes driving along."

Then the new Initiator remembered when she had begun doing the spiritual exercises as a newcomer in ECK. All kinds of noises would interrupt her. Many times it was the whistle of a train. She realized that these supposedly random happenings were the outer manifestation of the Sound Current. It's almost as if trumpets were sounding for a great spiritual event.

If distractions take place just when you're doing this sacred initiation, understand that it's part of the joy of life trying to express itself at that particular moment.

Testing Secret Words

Someone asked about a secret word coming through as a picture or a symbol. Generally you can ask people to reduce it to a one- or two-syllable word, whatever is called for at the initiation.

If they have a clear symbol, tell them, "Don't tell me what it is. You have the first step. Try to reduce it to a word, then test it." They themselves have to come up with a word. The Inner Master has given them this symbol for a reason—it's not an arbitrary thing.

Sacred Privilege

Don't give so many initiations that you're numb to the spiritual currents which are activated. If this happens, you're losing a remarkable experience for yourself. Enjoy the fullness of the experience.

Never forget the sacred privilege that surrounds the rite of initiation. It's such a blessing. An initiation not only uplifts the person receiving it, but it uplifts the Initiator, too. It's a renewal of one's spiritual life.

We've set up the RESA structure along hierarchical lines so that the message of ECK can come through as purely as possible. That way we're not constantly tripping over ourselves trying to figure out whether to go right, left, or straight ahead.

11

Working with
the Spiritual Hierarchy

On a plane trip to Europe, my wife and I sat down in a row with three seats across. Our seat companion came in, climbed over me with all his carry-on baggage, and sat in the window seat. He looked at me once then fell asleep for the rest of the flight.

We were about to land when all of a sudden this person started to act a little funny. He laughed to himself, then he was quiet. Then he started to laugh again, then he was quiet again. When we were just above the runway, he leaned over and said, "Excuse me, are you Harold Klemp?"

I said I was. He relaxed and sat back. The man beside me was an ECKist. I had said something to him when he sat down, but he hadn't really noticed me. Then just as we were landing he woke up inside. He told me, "It's a good thing I didn't know it was you sooner. I would have talked your ear off."

While we were landing, I asked him how he got into ECK. He said that over ten years ago an ECKist had given him *ECKANKAR—The Key to Secret Worlds*. He had enjoyed the book, but he wasn't ready for a commitment. Just in the last few years he was, and now he was a Second Initiate.

When you've given up everything of yourself and your own opinions, then you are finally ready to be a vehicle for the ECK. Until then, you're just getting used to yourself in your own surroundings.

What Do You Want Us to Do?

The first year the now retired ECK Spiritual Council worked together, they asked me, "What do you want us to do?" I said, "You'll know what to do when the time comes." They were all set to run out and do things. The second year they were not so frantic; they started to settle in to the role of the Spiritual Council. Now they were getting closer to what the ECK wanted.

At the next seminar, we met again. They said, "You know, we finally figured it out. We really don't have to do anything." So then I gave them work to do.

I would like to provide an opportunity—for you as Higher Initiates, for anyone who is at all interested— to get the most experience out of life. So that if you have talents of any kind, when you leave this earth you can say, "I've done it. I've done my best." I want to provide a climate where this can be experienced.

If ever a path had a rocky start, ECKANKAR is it. For at least a couple of centuries, a lot of credit will be given to the individuals, such as you, who helped make it possible. Sometimes you may look at the outer organization and shake your head. The fact is, behind all the illusionary fabrication and everything else, the Sound and the Light are stronger in ECK than in any other path on earth.

90

The RESA Structure

A RESA said to me, "It's really an interesting feeling these days when someone calls up and tells me he has a problem. He says he went to the inner and was told to call the RESA instead of the ECKANKAR Spiritual Center."

The RESAs are replicas of the Living ECK Master with limited authority. They're already taking over many of the responsibilities that used to come into the ECK office. A transition is already beginning on the inner planes.

This shouldn't make a RESA feel big and proud; it should make him feel humble and grateful to be a part of the spiritual works of ECK, working directly with the ECK.

The RESA structure is the means to reach the most people so they can get the experiences which are introductory to ECK. There are many people to reach during this particular period in history, people who someday will be in the same position as you are today. They are ready, and this is the time for it to be done.

Eventually we'll have a more introductory level in ECKANKAR for people who are getting their first real taste of ECK. In future lives they will be ready to move more rapidly into the inner circles of the Second to Eighth initiations.

Benefits of a Hierarchy

We had to make a choice when we were setting up the RESA field program. So that I could get the things accomplished which I am to do, we decided on a hierarchy. We have a spiritual precedent for this in the teachings of ECK—the spiritual hierarchy of the Order of the Vairagi. All the way down, the level above gives directions to the level below.

The other form we had considered was congregational. This means that the local Satsang would vote on administrative and even spiritual issues. Soon we would have an ECKANKAR organization that was divided roughly into three parts: those who felt we should be for something, those who felt we should be against something, and those who couldn't make up their minds.

If we'd introduce a second, then a third issue, soon there would be no strength in this organization to accomplish any of my mission. We would be totally helpless.

So we discarded the congregational form and chose the hierarchical. This way, when a direction comes from me to the local area, the RESA may ask the advice of the Satsang Society board, but the RESA still has the final word. I'm holding the RESAs responsible for helping me accomplish my mission.

When I meet with the Board of Trustees, they make suggestions, bring up problems, and offer solutions. But it is my place to say, "It is a good plan" or "It is not the best plan because it overlooks this spiritual principle."

What if a plan you present is rejected? It probably had weaknesses you couldn't see because of the limits in your own consciousness. The remedy? Contemplate more. Go to the Inner Master and say, "What did I overlook in my own plan? What have the others seen in the other plan that makes it a better one?"

We've set up the RESA structure along hierarchical lines so that the message of ECK can come through as purely as possible. That way we're not constantly tripping over ourselves trying to figure out whether to go right, left, or straight ahead.

Different Levels of Consciousness

Consciousness is individual and unique. Even among the Masters there are different levels of consciousness. You can speak of higher levels of consciousness, but you can also speak of scope or breadth of consciousness.

However high individuals are on the spiritual ladder, each also has a dimension of breadth, or scope. How broadly one can see is not necessarily related to how high he is on the ladder.

The Mahanta's Helpers

Today we are a global teaching for the first time in literally ages. Civilization on earth has progressed farther than ever in the past. There are also twice as many people walking the earth today as when I was born. That means there are twice as many chickens in the henhouse. If you know anything about chickens, when you start crowding them, you have problems. This crowding of people on earth is speeding up the spiritual evolutionary process.

Some chelas have felt a need for psychotherapy or counseling. Some Higher Initiates have said go ahead, but others saw it as an intrusion into the works of ECK. They felt one should simply ask the Mahanta and the Mahanta would take care of any emotional problems. But these chelas, rightly, see counselors as helpers of the Mahanta.

We're all too aware of the problems of daily life. But sometimes we're not able to make the jump ourselves to a detached state. Sometimes we need assistance.

Since You Asked

One time Paul Twitchell mentioned, "Because you ask, I can answer. And because I have to answer, I can give answers that otherwise I wouldn't be able to."

He was saying that working with chelas is a learning experience for him too. When the ECK spoke through him, he was also the detached observer and got the benefit of his own answer. A whole new field of knowledge could open up to him based on a question someone asked or a dream experience someone sent in, in an initiate report.

I Am My Own Master

Some Higher Initiates say, "I am my own master." They talk about working toward their own mastership. But often these are the people who have the hardest time in their own lives. They have the hardest time dealing with others. That should say something right there. They're out of sync, out of tune with the ECK, but they don't know it.

They don't really want to say it exactly, but they'd like everyone to believe that they are already ECK Masters. They're just waiting for me to confirm it, but I'm wondering if I should recommend them for psychotherapy or counseling.

Masters-in-Training

There are two circles in the SUGMAD world on the Twelfth Plane made up of ECK Masters who are candidates to be the Living ECK Master. Not every ECK Master wants to be—some excuse themselves and keep serving elsewhere. But there may be fifty or sixty in active training in one circle, trying to get into the inner circle—the candidates from which the SUGMAD chooses.

It's always the Will of the SUGMAD as It comes down through the different members of the hierarchy. They say, "With your skills, you seem to fit the times," and then you do it.

Between the time that a Living ECK Master leaves and the next October 22, his position will be taken by the Maharaji, the one appointed to receive the Rod of ECK Power on October 22. At this point he has the physical power and the physical responsibilities, but he is not ready to wear the crown. So Rebazar Tarzs carries the spiritual mantle until October 22. With the Rod of ECK Power this passes on to the next person.

The new Living ECK Master will unfold very quickly into the role of Mahanta. Although he's no child when he comes in as a Twelfth Initiate, he'll be sitting and watching, because it takes a long time to pick up all the reins for the duties that have to be done.

What the Mahanta Really Is

The real function of the Mahanta in this world is to maintain its balance. I may have goals, but really I'm working with the unfoldment of each person. As I do this, I watch the overall balance.

It's important to emphasize what the Mahanta actually is and what your relationship with the Mahanta is.

The Living ECK Master may have the Mahanta working through him and be called the Mahanta. The Mahanta works through such a person, but the Mahanta is never a person. The Mahanta is the ECK Itself, and

It takes on a form in different times. An important distinction: It's the difference between worship of the personality and truth.

Spiritual Specialists

The ECK Masters have a hierarchy from number one all the way down. No one in that organization is jealous of anyone who stands higher on the ladder as far as functional position goes. Spiritually, they know there is no difference. The man who pushes the broom doesn't worry if someone else happens to push a pen. There isn't any need for jealousy. It's pure love and service for God, which after all is only for yourself as a spark of God.

The ECK Masters are actually specialists in different fields. This is the meaning of the word *co-worker*— we pool our specialties and work together with harmony and cooperation. When we work together, there's no force greater than the brotherhood of ECK Masters or the Brothers of the Leaf.

When you have served enough, then you earn the next infusion of Light and Sound. That's a special experience, and when it comes there is just no question about the enlightenment. This is what gives you the strength to truly love someone else.

12

Learning about Love

As we unfold to any degree, we are no longer able to separate ourselves from our fellow human beings in even the smallest way. Even if we're shut in at home, there's a need to pass along the love of ECK that comes through the Spiritual Exercises of ECK.

Service with Love

First is often the dream state, then Soul Travel, then the Sound and the Light. Then comes service for the love of God, for the love of the SUGMAD. People who don't really have the Sound and Light can't understand why I'm always talking about service.

It's service with love, because you can't help it.

When you have served enough, then you earn the next infusion of Light and Sound. That's a special experience, and when it comes there is just no question about the enlightenment. This is what gives you the strength to truly love someone else.

Greener Grass

Some Higher Initiates have been in ECK for fourteen to twenty years, and they say, "I've been patient, but I haven't had any experiences." Generally they have had experiences. But the grass is always greener on the other side of the fence.

If they have dream experiences, they want Soul Travel. They have dream experiences because that is where they belong. But because they haven't had Soul Travel experiences, they totally overlook their dream experiences.

People who have Soul Travel experiences say, "I haven't had any experiences in the Light and Sound of God." They discount their dream and Soul Travel experiences.

This group generally lacks self-discipline. They're never satisfied with what they have, which isn't bad in itself. But they don't recognize the good things that they do have. They have no way of assessing their spiritual progress, of looking back and saying, "This is where I used to be, and this is where I am today."

It's usually because they won't do their spiritual exercises. They won't exercise their creativity in making new spiritual exercises. And because they don't, they aren't able to recognize the experiences they are having. So they're always looking at what they don't have, not at what they do have.

If you're without self-discipline, without right discernment, you point fingers at someone else and say, "That is why I fail."

Blessings of Giving

I like to give you as much opportunity as possible to give of yourselves. You unfold as a consequence of giving.

If you have the love and the willingness to work with

each other, begin practicing the concepts of co-workership. Do it with a heart full of love. I don't see how you can work together without love. If you're full of love when you work with each other, it just builds and builds.

You really can't separate giving love and getting love. They go hand in hand. Once one starts, the other comes.

This is where we always end up—with love.

Redefining Love

Life has unity. There is a cohesiveness that binds life from one end to the other, and this cohesiveness is love. We have been so used to defining love from the human consciousness that the definition needs redefining. We must first respect and love ourselves before we can respect and love another.

Sometimes we are more willing to harm and criticize each other than to get along with or love each other. Spiritually, we may not always agree. If you can't, just observe the Law of Silence. Write to me, if you will. If you see something that's not as it should be, I may look at it.

Divine love does not impose itself on another person. It allows others to live, move, and have their being.

Loving Other People

As Higher Initiates, you have to realize that the higher you go spiritually, the less able you are to make changes as quickly as you would like. This is because of the spiritual harm you could do to someone else.

Life is here to teach you to become a more loving, spiritual being. It can't be done by putting you into loving situations all the time. People become very self-ish in that atmosphere. After all, that's where Soul was in a way, if you can speak of Soul on the higher planes being selfish. It hadn't learned to give. And that's why we're here.

What these experiences do is bring you an over-whelming love for all living creatures. It doesn't mean indiscriminate love—if a cat scratches you, you'll probably waive your love for all life and push the cat away. But generally speaking—as long as nobody drops anything on your toe—you have this overwhelming love for all life.

When we have a realization about life and about the love of ECK, we sometimes forget this way may not be for another. If it is for another person, maybe it's better for him to catch ECK from your example rather than hearing about It from you directly. Maybe he has to see ECK at work in your life, rather than be told about It.

Loving God

I used to say, "Declare yourself a vehicle for the SUGMAD, the ECK, and the Mahanta." That's good, but I think there's something better. It's simply to say, "I love the SUGMAD, the ECK, and the Mahanta" as a declaration at the beginning of the day. This way you're not waiting like an empty saucepan for somebody to put something in—as if you're not Soul, not something worthwhile.

If you say, "I love the SUGMAD, the ECK, and the Mahanta," this means you're in a state of being. You are Soul, and you are a unit of love, whether you are doing something consciously or unconsciously.

The highest state of Soul is to be in love with

SUGMAD. This is the whole basis for the teachings of ECK. Not Soul Travel, not the dream state. The Light and Sound, but only because they are love.